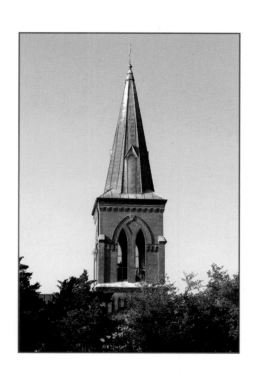

In gratitude for my lifelong friends
Jeff Rohr and Dick Jorgensen.

Library of Congress
Cataloging-in-Publication Data

Hanson, Warren.
  The steeple / written and illustrated by Warren Hanson.
    pages cm
  ISBN 978-0-931674-47-1 (alk. paper)
  I. Title.
  PS3608.A853S84 2013
  813'.6--dc23
                                             2013003994
  Author photo by Vera Matson Photography.

TRISTAN Publishing, Inc.
2355 Louisiana Avenue North
Golden Valley, MN 55427

Please visit us at:
www.tristanpublishing.com
books with a message

The Steeple

story and photographs by
Warren Hanson

TRISTAN Publishing
Minneapolis

First Christian Church, Edmond, Oklahoma

The morning I was born, my mother said,

was so sunny that it made the morning shine.

And she saw, outside the window from her bed,

a steeple. And she took it as a sign.

She said, "My darling baby, born today,

in life, so full of blessings, you will learn

that choices must be made along the way,

and sometimes you won't know which way to turn.

You may not always have me by your side,

but you will always have a steeple as your guide."

6

Venersborg Church
Battle Ground, Washington

A few weeks later, I was draped in white

as gathered family held hands and smiled

to witness the sweet sacramental rite —

the baptizing of earth and heaven's child.

The people there surrounded me with love,

as water trickled down, and words were said,

and ancient grace descended from above

beneath a steeple, smiling overhead.

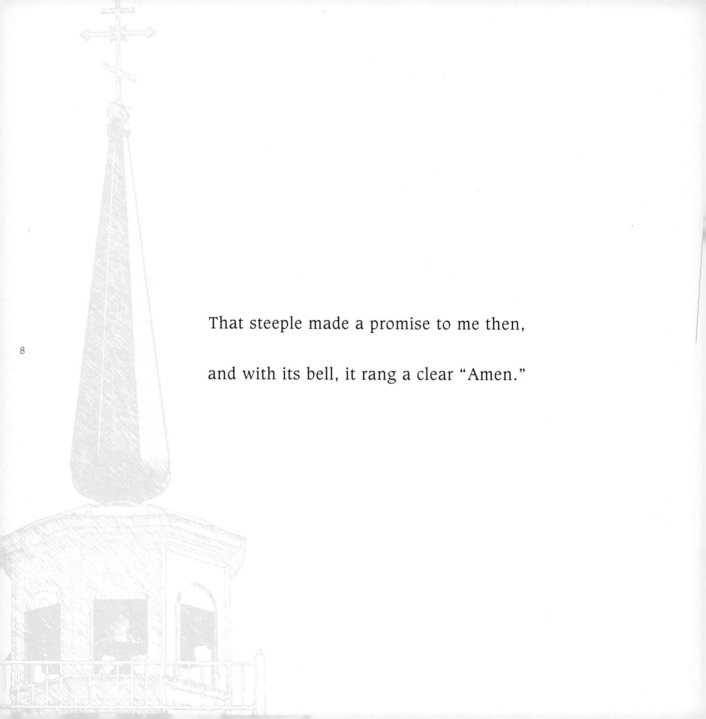

8

That steeple made a promise to me then,

and with its bell, it rang a clear "Amen."

St. Michael the Archangel
Russian Orthodox
Sitka, Alaska

First Presbyterian Church, Plattsburgh, New York

My childhood ran on magic, and on dreams,

adventure filling endless summer days

with hide-and-seek, and pick-up stickball teams,

and home-made costumes worn in made-up plays.

The kites flew high! The spinning pinwheels whirled!

And soapy bubbles bounced around the sky.

I didn't have a worry in the world,

as day by youthful day went flying by.

I conquered countless undiscovered lands,

with castles, kings, and chasms to be crossed.

I'd leap the moon, and brave the desert sands

with never any fear of getting lost.

Ste. Marie Catholic Church, Manchester, New Hampshire

And when I'd hear my mother's distant call

for supper, I would know the day was done.

I'd turn... and see it – faithful, straight and tall –

a beacon, lit with late afternoon sun.

It never mattered how far I would roam.

The steeple would be there to guide me home.

15

Stowe Community Church
Stowe, Vermont

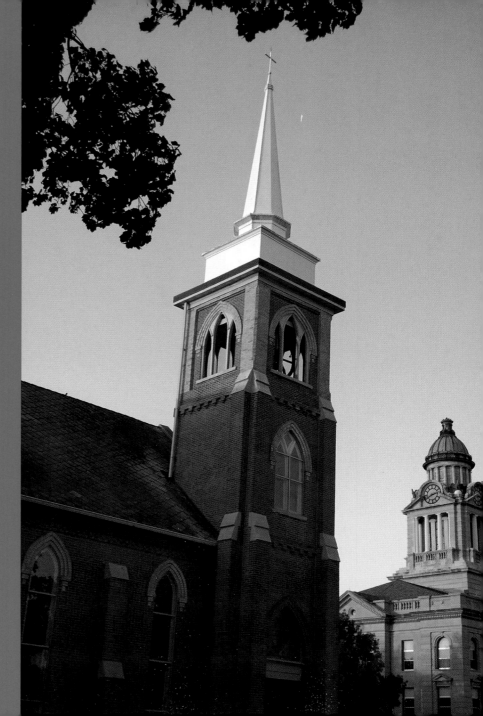

16

First United Methodist Church
Decorah, Iowa

But as I grew, I felt a growing doubt.

I questioned everything that I'd been told.

I wondered what the world was all about,

and swore that wisdom's wasted on the old.

Antioch Baptist Church, Shreveport, Louisiana

I started trying things I knew were wrong.

I challenged all adult authority.

I trashed what I had treasured all along

and turned my back on everything but me.

What I had once looked up to now seemed small.

A steeple's made by people, after all.

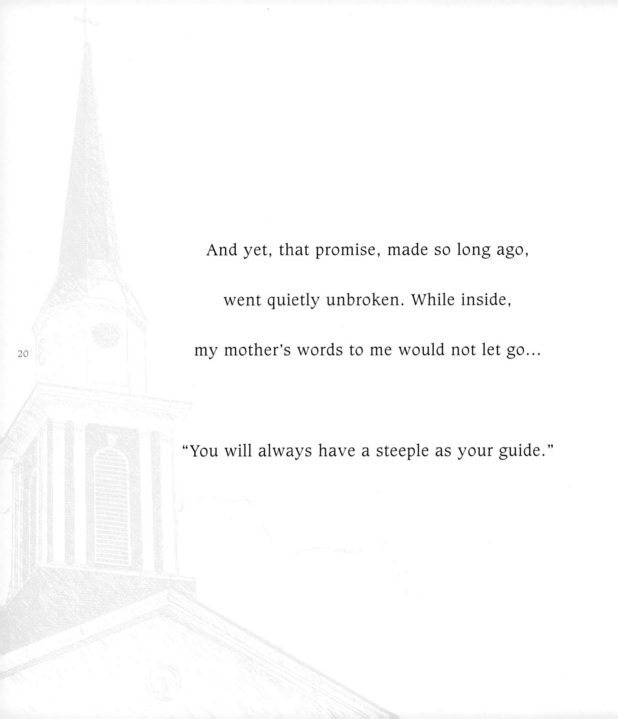

And yet, that promise, made so long ago,

went quietly unbroken. While inside,

my mother's words to me would not let go...

"You will always have a steeple as your guide."

First United Methodist Church
Magnolia, Arkansas

And she was right. A few years later on

I saw life differently. The remnants of

my teen rebellion mercifully were gone.

My heart turned happily to thoughts of love.

Notre Dame Catholic Church, Cresco, Iowa

First Congregational Church, Stockbridge, Massachusetts

And soon I knew that I had found the one

and only one with whom I wished to share

a brand new life. And so it was begun,

with family and friends all gathered there.

We held each other's hand, and with a smile

we walked, beneath the steeple, down the aisle.

Then... life got busy! Almost overnight!

New job. New house. New baby on the way.

And then another one. No end in sight

to all that needed doing every day!

"Can you please change this diaper? I'm on hold

with someone who says he can fix the roof."

"The babysitter called. She has a cold

and can't...

Stop that! The cat's not waterproof!"

Old Scandinavian Church
Yankton, South Dakota

Old South Meeting House, Boston, Massachusetts

"That meeting at the church tomorrow night

is at the same time as the one at school."

"Oh, there's the doorbell..."

"Hey, I said don't fight!"

"I'm sorry. Sometimes I just lose my cool."

30

Grace Episcopal Church
Stafford Springs, Connecticut

"Did anyone see where I put my keys?"

"Okay, I'll call the plumber right away!"

"Can someone make that dog stop barking, PLEASE?!"

"Of course I love you."

"Huh? What did you say?

Well, how on earth would keys get under there?"

"What? A steeple? Oh, I'm sure it's here somewhere..."

St. Mary, Star of the Sea Catholic Church, Astoria, Oregon

Our life was always being rearranged,

while I tried haplessly to set it right.

Then...

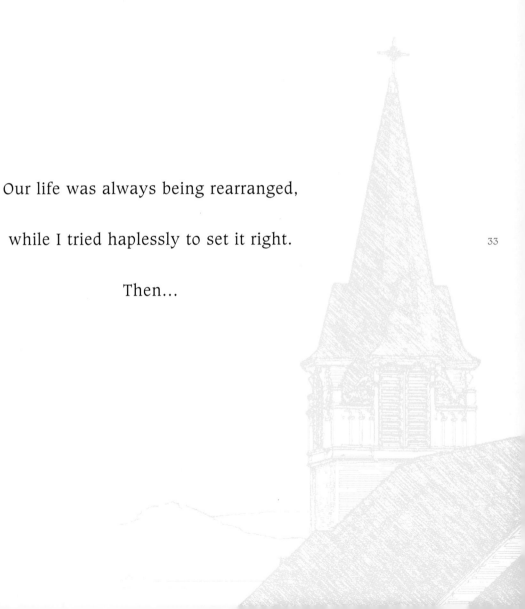

...in a minute, everything was changed

by an unexpected phone call in the night.

St. Anne's Catholic Church, Houston, Texas

The voice I'd known from birth had now gone still.

That voice that spoke so wisely to me when

I needed guidance, as I always will.

Now, I would never hear that voice again.

St. Mary Catholic Church
Ellinger, Texas

38

Beth Immanuel
Sabbath Fellowship
Hudson, Wisconsin

I stood there in the darkness all alone,

as quiet tears ran slowly down my face.

The news I'd just been given on the phone

had sent me to another time and place.

A sunny morning, many years ago.

A young new mother, lying in her bed,

would look into the light, and she would know

that one day I'd remember what she said...

"You may not always have me by your side,

but you will always have a steeple as your guide."

United Church of Northfield, Northfield, Vermont

Then, as I stood reflecting on that day,

I saw outside my window in the night

a steeple, standing not so far away,

at peace beneath the moon's consoling light.

I'd never noticed, so I could be wrong...

but that steeple must have been there all along.

*Christ Episcopal Church
Newcastle, Wyoming*

Helvetia Community Church, Hillsboro, Oregon

44

We live our lives in hope that we will know

the best direction each and every day,

when often we're not sure which way to go

and wish someone were there to show the way.

For me, when I don't know which way to turn,

I listen for that voice I've known so well,

the wisdom that encouraged me to learn

to listen for that distant ringing bell.

That gentle voice. That promise, here inside...

Central Lutheran Church
Minneapolis, Minnesota

I will always have a steeple as my guide.

Stories Behind the Photographs

front cover:

First Lutheran Church, Decorah, IA

My wife Becky's parents lived the last years of their lives in Decorah, and they are buried there. First Lutheran sits on top of a tree-covered hill and looks down over the town. This is the view from across the Upper Iowa River.

p.1:

St. Mary Catholic Church, High Hill, TX

This is one of the famous Painted Churches of Fayette County, which have elaborately painted interiors done by itinerant artists in the early 1900s. I preferred shooting my photos in the early morning light, so I didn't get to see the interior because the church wasn't open yet. But the steeple can be seen for miles around.

p.4:

First Christian Church, Edmond, OK

The clean lines of this simple steeple against the clear, unclouded sky seemed the perfect symbol of the morning of birth that starts the story. But I loved the pealing paint on the louvres around the belfry, a reminder that there is no such thing as actual perfection.

p.6:

Venersborg Church, Battle Ground, WA

I planned a trip to the Pacific Northwest, partly to search for steeples, but mostly to visit my daughter Lacey in Portland, Oregon.

Vancouver, Washington, is just on the other side of the Columbia River from Portland, so I planned to try to find some steeples there. But all of my Google searching produced very meager results. I kept widening my search, until I found this rustic church outside the town of Battle Ground. But even though there were a few pictures of the church online, I had some questions. So I called the pastor. Which direction does the church face? Does it catch sunlight at any time during the day? Is there a bell in the steeple? He said that, yes, there is a bell, but it sits up very high, so it's hard to see. And the only time the church gets direct sunlight is early in the morning.

I arrived at 5:00 a.m. It was still completely dark. In order to get the shot I wanted, I had to set my tripod right in the middle of the two-lane highway in front of the church. I had to hope that a car wouldn't come along and hit me in the dark. I sat patiently on the cold pavement until the morning started to brighten. But the sky dawned cloudy, so I wouldn't be getting any direct sunlight. I started shooting, and took a shot every few seconds as the sky grew light. Fortunately, no cars came by.

p.9:

St. Michael the Archangel, Russian Orthodox, Sitka, AK

When we went on an Alaskan cruise in July of 2011, I was already well into the steeples project. So I had my eye out for steeples that were unique to that area. This one was perfect.

St. Michael the Archangel burned to the ground in 1966, but was meticulously rebuilt from the original plans. This photo, with the bells clearly showing, seemed just right to go with the text "and with its bell, it rang a clear 'Amen'."

p. 10:

First Presbyterian Church, Plattsburgh, NY

My wife and I took a ferry across Lake Champlain from Vermont on a gorgeous, sunny morning. This statuesque steeple stands in downtown Plattsburgh. I was very pleased to get this shot, with that cloud playing hide-and-seek in the distance, and no power lines in the way. Power lines were the biggest problem I faced in getting all the photos for this book.

p. 13:

Ste. Marie Catholic Church, Manchester, NH

I had found this wonderful steeple by searching online. I liked the castle-like fairytale appearance of it. It sits on a hill across the river from downtown Manchester, just like a castle would. When I got home and started sorting through my images, I thought that this would work well with the section of the story that talks about the fanciful, imaginative, care-free play of childhood. So I paired it with the words in the story about having adventures and leaping the moon. It was only later that I realized that the moon is actually in the picture!

p. 15:

Stowe Community Church, Stowe, VT

This is one of the most photographed churches in America. And it's easy to see why. Sitting as it does in the wooded hills of Vermont, no one would ever guess that it actually faces the busy main street of downtown Stowe. Just out of sight, among those trees, are dozens of bustling shops and restaurants.

It is also the most photographed steeple of my entire project. I took nearly 100 pictures of this church -- in early morning, bright afternoon, dusky evening, from high and from low, from right and from left. But when I matched this photo with the text that said "faithful, straight and tall -- a beacon, lit with late afternoon sun," I knew that this was just the right shot.

p. 16:

First United Methodist Church, Decorah, IA

We were in Decorah to bury the ashes of Becky's brother right next to where their parents are buried. We stayed in a B&B, and this church was right across the street. I took this shot on an evening walk with our dog Scout, not really knowing if I would use it or not.

But when I looked at the shot later, I realized that it was just right for the rebellious teen section of the story I was writing. This steeple looks like it is challenging authority, as it leans defiantly in the direction of the courthouse across the street.

51

p.18:

Antioch Baptist Church, Shreveport, LA

I planned a day to take a driving trip into Louisiana and Arkansas to look for steeples. I left home at 4:00 a.m. for what turned out to be a 14-hour day of driving.

I found this brooding, dark brick church in a very poor part of town. Though I believe that it may still be in use, it had a feeling of abandonment. The heavy clouds of night were just starting to break up in the morning sun. I noticed that the openings in the belfry had been bricked up, and I realized that this might be perfect for the part of the story that talks about the sullen teen years. This steeple is closed off, unwilling to listen. So I shot it from an angle that felt like it has its back turned to us, kind of moody and rebellious, like a teenager.

This church, dating from the late 1800s, is on the National Register of Historic Places.

p.21:

First United Methodist, Magnolia, AR

In planning my trip into Arkansas in search of steeples, I called one of the other churches in Magnolia to ask if their church had a steeple. The secretary said it did not. So I asked if she knew of any churches with steeples in town. She said, "I think the Methodist Church might have one." Magnolia is a small town, and this church is at its center. I'm sure that woman drives past this steeple every day without noticing it. I think we all do that.

p.23:

Notre Dame Catholic Church, Cresco, IA

There are beautiful churches in very small towns throughout the United States. This one stands just off the main street of Cresco, Iowa. With its head held high, facing the morning sun, it seemed to reflect the sunny optimism of the text across the page.

p.24:

First Congregational, Stockbridge, MA

This is the steeple that caused me to start working on this book in earnest. For years I'd had the idea of writing a story about steeples and their significance in our lives, but at this point the idea was still pretty vague. Becky and I had gone to Massachusetts for the opening of a show of a friend's illustration work at the Norman Rockwell Museum in Stockbridge. This steeple is such a New England classic that it reminded me of the story idea I'd been holding onto for so long.

p.27:

Old Scandinavian Church, Yankton, SD

This is the church my family attended when I was born. I liked the interesting detail of the steeple, and I even liked the weathered texture of the peeling paint and deteriorating roof.

Later I realized that this would be a good photo to use in that comical section of the story where the narrator is on hold, waiting to talk with someone who says he will come and fix the roof. Sadly, this church was torn down shortly after I took this photograph.

p.28:

Old South Meeting House, Boston, MA

Many of the protest meetings that led to the Boston Tea Party in 1773 were held beneath this steeple. And here it still stands, against the backdrop of a modern glass-and-steel city, a good photo for "that meeting at the church."

p.30:

Grace Episcopal, Stafford Springs, CT

I had done my homework, and had planned on photographing the steeple of Stafford Springs Congregational Church. But when I got there, I found that there were too many power lines too close to the church for me to get a good shot. As I walked around and around the church, I spotted another steeple a few blocks away. And it was kind of unique. So I walked over to take a look. I liked the steeple, and there were no power lines in the way!

But when I lifted my camera to start shooting, I found that I had let my battery go dead. Fortunately, I had my little point-and-shoot camera in the car. It's a great little camera, and it did a good job of getting the shot I wanted.

And, yes, that is the steeple of Stafford Springs Congregational Church in the background. And a few of those pesky power lines.

p.32:

St. Mary, Star of the Sea Catholic Church, Astoria, OR

This church sits in a lovely spot, on a hillside overlooking the Columbia River. But in order to get the shot I wanted, I had to climb even higher on that hillside and stand in someone's sloping front yard, hoping they wouldn't come out and tell me to get off their property. The grass was wet and slippery with morning dew, and I ended up sliding down that front yard on my bottom, trying hard to protect the camera.

I had first been intrigued by the name of this church. But I hadn't been able to see pictures of it on Google, because apparently this is a fairly new building and location. (My GPS kept taking me to the wrong place.) But once I found it, I fell in love with the detailed steeple. And this view makes it look almost as though it has forlorn eyes. I decided to use it in that part of the story that says, "while I tried haplessly..."

This was shot on a Sunday morning, and there were services going on inside at the time. I could hear the people singing.

p.35:

St. Anne's Catholic Church, Houston, TX

I had planned this moonlit shot very carefully ahead of time. But this is not the shot I'd planned.

July 3, 2012, would have a full moon. I wanted to take advantage of that and get a shot of a steeple by moonlight. I had searched

53

Google to find an urban church in Houston that had a beautiful, or at least interesting, steeple. I discovered Annunciation Catholic Church.

But on July 3, the weather didn't cooperate. So I hoped for a clear sky on July 4, when the moon would still be almost full. But Becky reminded me of the big fireworks show in downtown Houston, and she really didn't want me to get into all that traffic. So I got up at 3:00 a.m. on July 5 and drove downtown. With the help of Google Street View, I had planned just how to find the church, where I would park, and where I would set up my tripod to get the shot I wanted. Downtown Houston was deserted. I turned the last corner to find the church, looked up, and saw that the entire steeple was encased in scaffolding for repairs! Now what?

I got out my iPhone and started looking up other churches nearby. But I found no steeples worth shooting. So I just started driving around aimlessly. I was almost ready to head home when I saw this gorgeous tower. I pulled over, jumped out, set up my tripod, and started shooting. I was inexperienced with shooting in the dark, so most of my shots ended up out of focus. But all it takes is one!

p.37:

St. Mary Catholic Church, Ellinger, TX

I had heard about a very old cemetery in this part of Texas where a country church was visible in the distance. I had hoped to get a shot to go with the death of the mother in the story. I couldn't find the cemetery, but I did find the church. I arrived just before sunrise, and I didn't see the graveyard at first. But when I did turn around and see it, I started saying out loud, "Oh, my gosh! Oh, my gosh!" I couldn't believe my good luck. It was perfect!

p.38:

Beth Immanuel Sabbath Fellowship, Hudson, WI

I knew that I was running out of time to get the photos I wanted for the book. And I needed a night shot to go along with the words, "I stood there in the darkness all alone." Night shots are very difficult to get, and I needed to get this right.

We were going to be in Minneapolis for the fall book show. I was trying to get photos in as many different states as possible, and I already had one from Minnesota. So I went to Google and looked for good steeples in Hudson. I chose this one because it is classic, but also unusual because the steeple has eight sides. I also liked it because this is the home of a Messianic Jewish community, and I liked the way that it reflected two aspects of the heritage of my publisher, Brett Waldman.

I saw on the congregation's website that they would have a service at 7:26 p.m. on the Saturday after the book show. It would give me an opportunity to get a shot as the sky got dark but there would be lights on inside. But there was also a country church near Amery that I wanted to shoot in morning light. So I got up at 4:00 a.m. on that Saturday and drove to Wisconsin. I decided to take a look at this steeple on my way to Amery, and I discovered that the interior lights were on! It was cold as I set up my tripod in the middle of the street and started shooting. I love the lonely moodiness of this shot. I never did make it to Amery.

p.41:

United Church of Northfield, Northfield, VT

On a drive through Vermont for a friend's wedding, my wife and I drove past a town called Northfield. She had gone to college in a town called Northfield (Minnesota). So early the next morning, before she was awake, I sneaked out and drove back to this town to get a photo of this classic New England steeple in the morning light. I didn't notice until later, when I was examining the photos closely, that someone had thrown a plastic wiffle ball onto the roof. I decided to leave it in the picture as a reminder that these steeples are surrounded by real life.

p.43:

Christ Episcopal Church, Newcastle, WY

This is the last photo I took for the project. I was going to be staying with friends in the Black Hills of South Dakota, and I knew that Newcastle was only a half-hour drive away. I needed a night shot, and I hoped that I might be lucky enough to also have a moon.

I woke up at 4:00 a.m. to drive to Newcastle. There were big, fat, wet flakes of snow falling, and I wondered if I would be able to get any kind of shot at all. But the snow cleared as I drove down out of the Hills. And though the sky was cloudy, the moon was peeking out from time to time.

I set up my tripod on the cold, wet grass in front of the church, sat down on that grass, and waited. I needed there to be a little bit of morning light in the sky, but not too much. I had to move a few inches every five minutes or so as the moon moved across the sky.

I was concentrating so hard on the sky and the light that I didn't notice that a cat had come up onto the porch of the church and was sitting there watching me. It wasn't until I got home and looked at the photos at full size that I realized he was there in almost every shot, until one that shows him going down the steps, on to more interesting activities.

Because of the cat and the moon and the sky and the memories, this might be my favorite shot in the book.

p.44:

Helvetia Community Church, Hillsboro, OR

While I was visiting my daughter Lacey in Portland, Oregon, she came with me on a day of "steeple chasing". This classic church is over 100 years old and is surrounded by farmland. The steeple was just right for the line in the story about a "distant ringing bell." This photo will always remind me of a wonderful day spent with my daughter.

55

p.46:

Central Lutheran Church, Minneapolis, MN

Some will say that, technically, this is a tower, not a steeple. I choose to overlook that technicality because, with its ornate majesty, in the bright morning sunlight, against the sky dappled with clouds, this shot provided exactly the positive, encouraging, and hopeful ending I wanted for the story.

p.48:

Glenwood Lutheran, rural Decorah, IA

I was so concerned about leaning across a barbed wire fence to get this shot that it wasn't until much later that I noticed the grand, billowing cloud that sets off this country steeple so beautifully.

back cover:

The Old Church, Portland, OR

I started taking pictures of this ornate steeple at 4:30 in the morning, hoping to get a shot of the steeple silhouetted against the sunrise. I sat on the cold sidewalk across the street for a couple of hours, taking picture after picture. But I didn't get what I wanted. I came back two more times during the day and finally captured its beautiful detail in the afternoon light.

I want to express my deep gratitude and appreciation for my wife Becky, who believed so strongly in this book, and who lovingly encouraged me as I went chasing steeples.

—WH